hand lettering & MODERN CALLIGRAPHY for Kids

Send us an email at

modernkidpress@gmail.com

to get an extra printable!

Just title the email "Lettering" and we will
send a surprise your way!

Hand Lettering and Modern Calligraphy for Kids

© Modern Kid Press

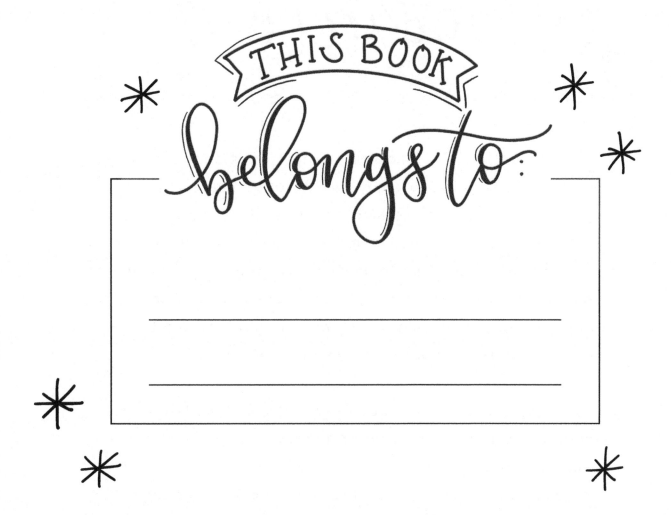

introduction

Hello there! I'm glad you picked up this book. I think you are really going to enjoy your time learning to letter! Wanna know my favorite thing about hand lettering? Each and every person is unique and so is their hand lettering style! You are beautifully uniquely you and I hope you come to find that your hand lettering is too! I hope that you find joy in the process of learning a new form of creativity and then use it to create art that reflects your own uniqueness!

Maybe you have already kicked off your hand lettering journey by writing your name on the previous page. If not, grab any writing utensil and go do that now! Don't wait until you think you've perfected your hand lettering. It'll be fun to see how much you've grown after you have practiced (and then practiced some more and more and more)!

I can't wait to get started on this journey with you!
Let's kick this thing off...

table of contents

getting started

TERMINOLOGY

If you're going to learn to letter, we've got to get through a bit of vocabulary words first so don't start skipping pages just yet!

DOWNSTROKE: Any movement downward with the writing instrument. These lines are thick!

UPSTROKE: Any movement upward with the writing instrument. These lines are thin!

ASCENDER: The part of the letter that extends above the mean line (i.e. the top portion of the 't' seen here).

DESCENDER: The part of the letter that falls below the baseline (i.e. the bottom portion of letters such as 'g' and 'y').

FLOURISH: These are the added strokes and swashes used to decorate or enhance letters.

CROSSBAR: Horizontal strokes on letters such as 't,' 'f,' and uppercase 'H'.

LETTERFORM: The form or shape of a letter.

TOOLS

While there are lots and lots of options out there, we're going to keep our lettering toolbox fairly simple to start out with! To get started, here are a few tools and materials to have on hand.

 KEY TO SUCCESS: Find a cute box to store all of your supplies... it's nice to have everything all in one place! You can decorate the outside once you've gotten some lettering practice under your belt!

 Crayola broad line markers are great for larger projects and the Crayola Super Tips work great for stationery and other small projects! And you can't beat the color variety in a good pack of markers!

 Colored pencils also work great for many lettering styles! Their fine tip is also great when you start adding fancy decorative elements to your letters, if your heart should so desire!

 Not to be left out is our good ole' box of crayons! A classic crayon-drawn letter leaves a pretty cool texture as well!

 Your favorite pencil will do, too! It's nice to have the option to erase and start over so be sure to add in a good soft eraser to your toolbox as well!

The thing about lettering is that you can write on just about any surface! While you're practicing, just grab any smooth finish white paper. When working on cards or invitations, it's also nice to have card stock on hand.

the how-to!

Let's start with three different classifications of lettering: serif, sans serif and script. These each have their own unique look and with the knowledge (and a lot of practice) of each one, you will be able to develop a wide range of lettering styles to suite a multitude of different projects! Here's a visual of each style...

The word 'serif' refers to the small decorative lines added to the end of a letterform's main strokes. It is known to be the easiest style of lettering to read!

Sans, meaning without, refers to letterforms that do not have a serif at the end of the letter's strokes.

Script is a fluid style of lettering where each letter is connected. Think cursive, but with a bit more flair!

Both the serif and sans serif styles above were created with a monoline stroke (another word for the line your draw with your pen!). Monoline just means that each stroke is the same thickness so all of the upstrokes and downstrokes look the same. See how the word 'script' above looks different? That's because I used a "faux calligraphy" method. More about that on the next page!

Scripted hand lettering looks a little bit different from monoline in that there is variation in the thickness of the upstrokes and downstrokes. It is sometimes called 'faux calligraphy' or 'fauxlligraphy' because it mimics the look of traditional calligraphy where thick and thin strokes are created by how hard you push down with those fancy old school calligraphy pens. Let's break it down into a simple three step process!

STEP 1: Draw in your letterform/word.

STEP 2: Draw in a secondary connecting downstroke.

STEP 3: Fill in those downstrokes!

Downstrokes are **thick**,
Upstrokes are thin.
Don't forget it!

warm-ups

Try tracing these shapes and then recreating them on your own to get your hand warmed up!

Hand lettering is basically a lot of muscle memory so the more you practice, the better you'll be!

Each of these basic shapes make up the majority of our letterforms so let's try combining a few! (Didn't know you'd be doing equations when you picked up this book, did ya?)

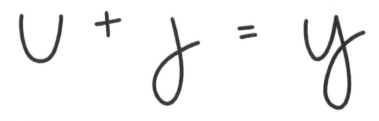

$$U + j = y$$

$$\ell + b = f$$

$$| + \wedge = n$$

Way to go! Let's start putting those addition skills to the test with the following alphabets!

alphabets

a b c d e f

g h i j k l

m n o p q

r s t u v

w x y z

Get ready, get set...... Our first alphabet practice is a lowercase hand lettered alphabet! This lettering style is best created with a marker or pen, in any size! Remember the golden rule we discussed earlier: downstrokes are thick and upstrokes are thin! We will practice each letter individually on the next few pages...

...and keep on going!

q q q

r r r

s s s

t t t

u u u

v v v

w w w

x x x

A B C D E F
G H I J K L
M N O P Q
R S T U V
W X Y Z

KEEP YOUR MARKER OR PEN IN HAND...... Now that you have warmed up with lowercase letters, let's move right along to uppercase! If you want to try a new tool out, switch things up and grab another! The more you practice, the more you will have a feel for what pens or markers you like working with best!

26

I *I* *I*

J *J* *J*

K *K* *K*

L *L* *L*

M *M* *M*

N *N* *N*

O *O* *O*

P *P* *P*

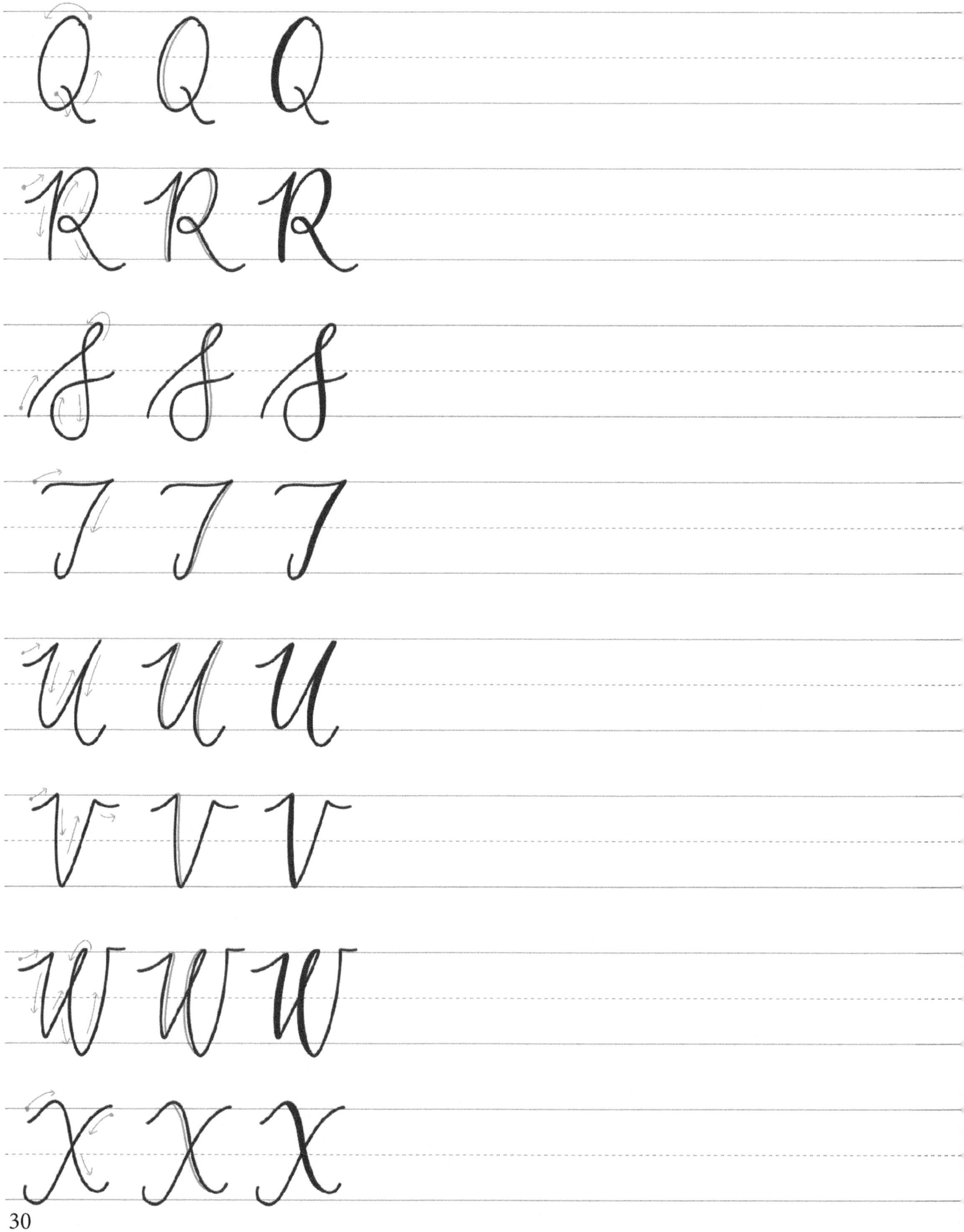

Q Q Q

R R R

S S S

T T T

U U U

V V V

W W W

X X X

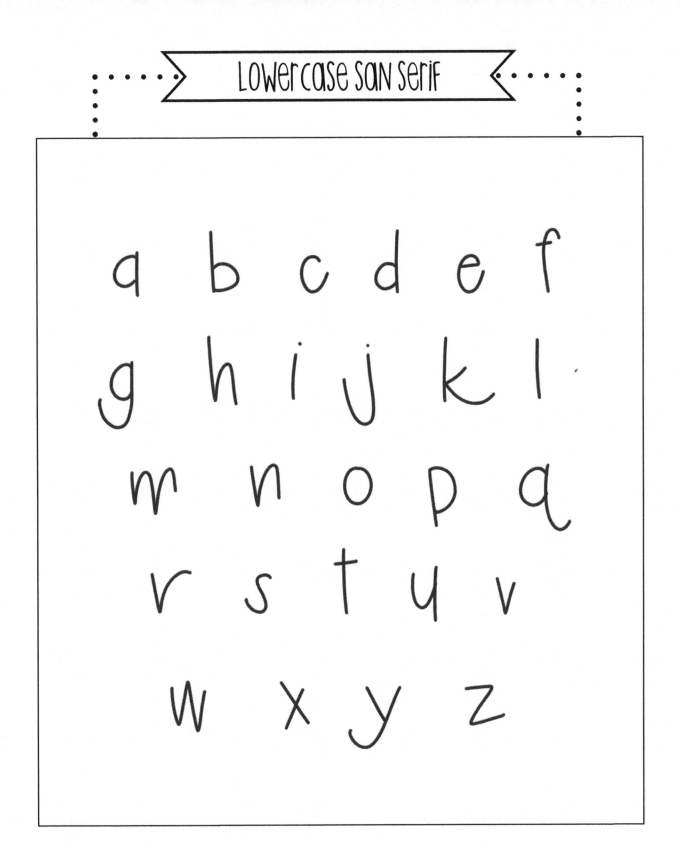

LOOK FAMILIAR?...... You have probably had the most practice with the san serif alphabet, right? Challenge yourself to think beyond your regular handwriting and picture each letter as art that you are creating line by line. With more practice, you will be able to change up the look of even the simplest of letters!

a

b

c

d

e

f

g

h

...and keep on going!

i

j

k

l .

m

n

o

p

y

z

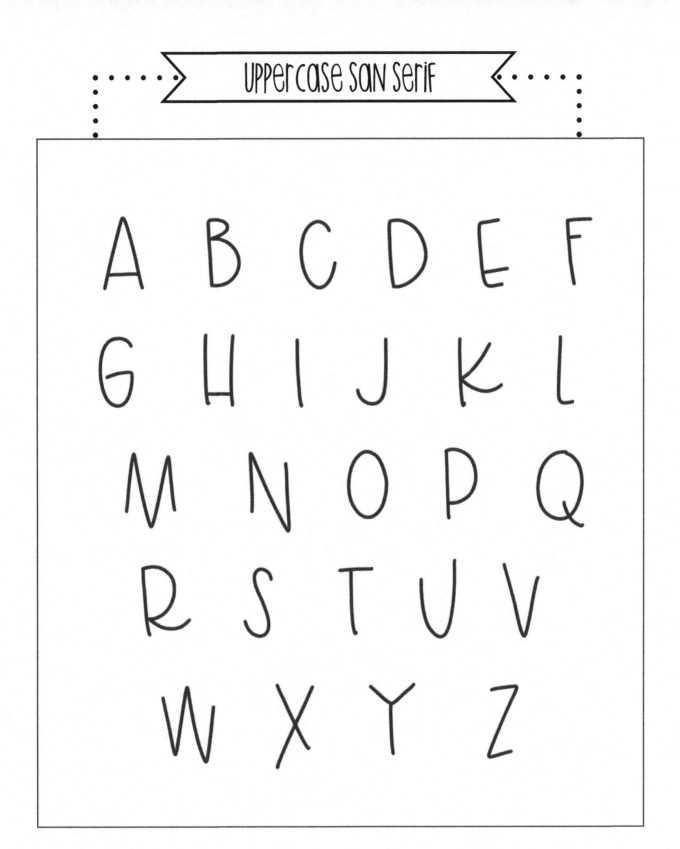

KEEP IT UP ... You're doing great! We are moving right along with the uppercase san serif alphabet.

A

B

C

D

E

F

G

H

Y

Z

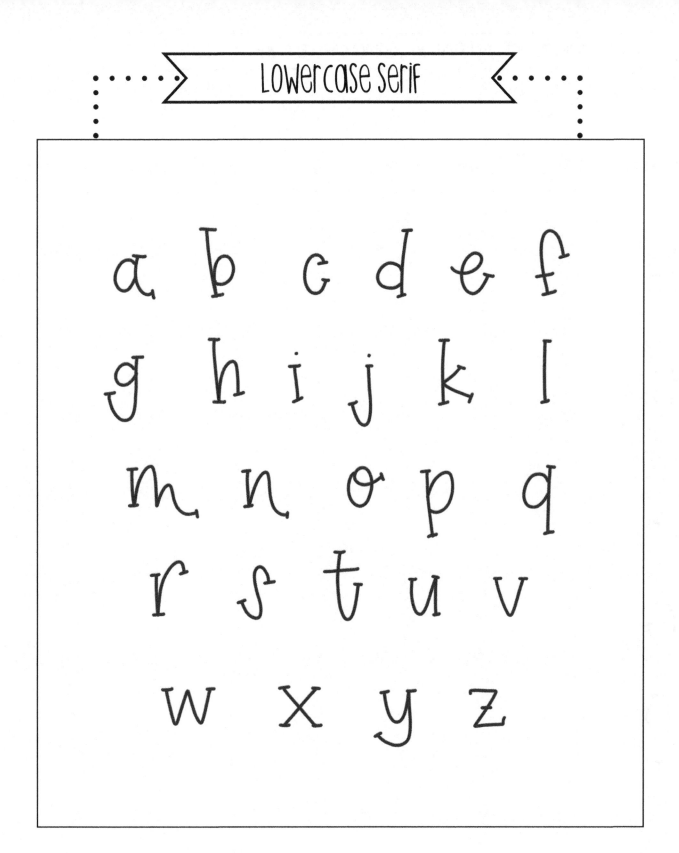

Change it up...... Take the san serif style that we previously worked on, and add those little lines to the end of your strokes to create the serif look!

a

b

c

d

e

f

g

h

i

j

k

l

m

n

o

p

y

z

A B C D E F

G H I J K L

M N O P Q

R S T U V

W X Y Z

LAST ONE...... Our final alphabet is the uppercase serif. Stay focused on creating each of your letters with uniform look. The repetitive motion of copying your letters over and over is building up muscle memory!

A

B

C

D

E

F

G

H

...and keep on going!

I

J

K

L

M

N

O

P

connecting

CONNECTIONS

Connecting your letters can be tricky to master, but it is also one of the most fun ways to develop your own style in hand lettering. The final upstroke of each letterform from our previous alphabet practice pages will become your connecting stroke between each letter. Although it is important to focus on each letter as an individual shape to keep your letterforms consistent, in time you will learn that it helps to always be thinking ahead to your next letter. These connecting strokes will create space between your letters. While learning, try and keep this space consistent between each letter. Work slowly and think ahead to the next letter so that you know where you are headed!

The example below walks through my thought process as I wrote out the phrase "let's get together."

Connecting the 'l' to the 'e' was a natural fit. The final upstroke of the 'l' blends into the same direction of the 'e' beginning upstroke.

Here, the final upstroke of the 'e' was extended upward to meet the thick downstroke of the 't.'

Instead of starting the 'o' with a slight upstroke, I simply brought the final upstroke of the 't' to meet the initial downstroke of the 'o.'

Because the end stroke of the 'e' and beginning stroke of the 'r' do not naturally line up, I raised up the letter 'r' to sit a little higher so that the letters would flow together seamlessly.

Let's make this a bit easier by breaking the words apart. Use these 3 steps with script lettering to get a feel for how to connect each letter natually.

Step 1: Start by writing out each individual letter with space in between.

get

Step 2: Look at the starting and ending strokes (or tails) of each letter. See how they tend to want to join naturally? Draw in small lines connecting each of the tails between each letter.

get

Step 3: Now try writing the scripted word as one fluid line without spaces in between!

get

Great job! Can you see how breaking it down into steps helps you see the flow from one letter to the next? Once you have practiced more, you can eliminate steps one and two and skip to writing the entire word at one time!

Let's try it on your own! I imagine one of the words you most frequently write is your own name, so let's start there!

Follow my lead...

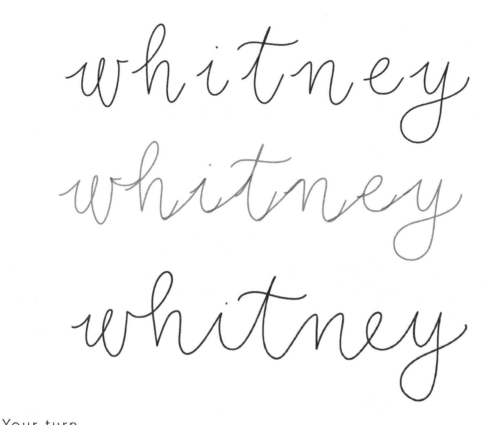

Your turn...

Now try writing your friend's names!

look @ U GO!

cool

kind

super

yippee

yay

rad

shine

dream

bright

beautiful

friends

brave

hello

hooray

love

sweet

fun

awesome

Practice a few words of your own!

creating your style

CREATING YOUR UNIQUE STYLE

I told you how much I love the uniqueness of individual lettering styles in the beginning of this book, so you can imagine how I feel about this section... Get ready to mix things up! Woo-hoo! Changing the look of the letters that we've been practicing on previous pages is easy with a few simple methods. Let's go over them...

SLANT // One easy way is by changing the angle of your letters. See the difference it made in the example below? The style on the top looks much more formal with a simple slant of the word.

Pick a few words or phrases of your own to try out on the next page!

 KEY TO SUCCESS: Put a piece of white copy paper on top of the next page to practice so you can keep the guideline clean and continue to use it over and over!

LOOP SIZE // Changing the shape and size of your ascender and descender loops can take a formal style and change it to more of a fun and whimsical lettering style. Consider what the purpose of your lettering is and what message you want to convey, then decide what look best fits!

For example: I might use smaller loops like the example below if I was addressing an envelope for a formal wedding invitation.

Miss Eleanor Rose

And the style below is a fun look for a birthday party or event invite!

Miss Eleanor Rose

Use the example for reference and try it out on your own!

NARROW

WIDE

FLOURISHES // Adding decorative curls and swashes to the ascenders, descenders and tails of your letters is a fun way to really elevate your style! Try these out and notice how it really changes the look of a letter.

Check out the difference in these two words. Which do you like more? Adding flourishes or keeping things simple is up to you!

Try these out on your own!

LETTER HEIGHT // It sounds simple but the height of your letters shapes the look of your hand lettered word as a whole. Picture each letter fitting inside of a box and filling the space entirely. Try it out below!

HEY

HEY

HEY

DECORATIVE LETTERS // Let's really add some flair with this next one! Pull out your favorite lettering tool and try out a few of these variations. What do you like? What look best says "I am me!"? As they say: you do you!! (Are they still saying that? I'm going to roll with it!)

DROP SHADOW // Add a thin line just to the right or left of each of your downstrokes to create a shadow effect. Try it out on your own in the space below...

OUTLINE // Draw a thin line (or 2) around your whole word. This effect really highlights a word making it stand out more in a design!

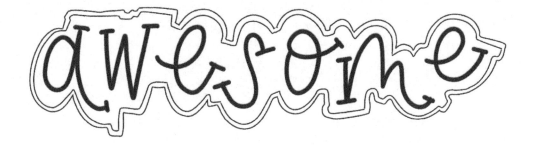

DOTTED OUTLINE // Try adding a dotted border around your word for a fun and playful look!

DOTTED INSIDE // Grab two different colors, one light and one dark to switch things up on this one! Use your light color to write your word in thick lettering, then add a dotted line inside in your dark color.

projects

Trace the design below then try it on your own!

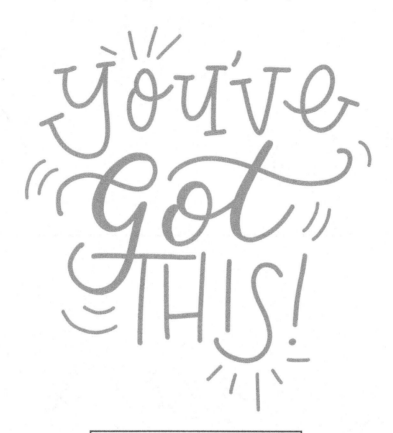

NOW YOU TRY!

Trace the design below then try it on your own!

NOW YOU TRY!

Monogram wall art! Trace the letter below, then practice on the page to the right with your own initial! Choose a simple pattern to fill the space around the circle. To make this artwork to hang on your wall, trace a circle onto a piece of cardstock then recreate your design!

Trace the design below then try it on your own!

NOW YOU TRY!

Trace the design below then try it on your own!

Good things AheAd ➡

NOW YOU try!

Trace the design below then try it on your own!

NOW YOU TRY!

Trace the design below then try it on your own!

NOW YOU TRY!

Trace the design below then try it on your own!

oh hey VACAY

NOW YOU TRY!

Trace the design below then try it on your own!

NOW YOU TRY!

Trace the design below then try it on your own!

NOW YOU TRY!

Trace the design below then try it on your own!

NOW YOU TRY!

let's celebrate

Well done! You made it through all of our projects! Now let's have some fun putting your skills to the test! One of my favorite ways to use my lettering skills is by making beautiful stationery and signage for birthday parties and other events. With a few simple supplies you can make all the decoration that you need.

Have a birthday coming up? A sleepover? A holiday themed party? Want to host a party for no reason at all? I hope these next few pages of projects will be a fun way to add to your party decor!

Gift Tags

Create fun gift tags to attach to any party favors you may have! Start by tracing the handlettered designs below, then trace the templates at the bottom of the page onto some cardstock, cut it out and add a word or phrase!
Here are a few ideas: Thanks for Coming, You Rock, You're the Best!

MATERIALS:
Cardstock
Scissors
Writing Utensil
Hole Punch

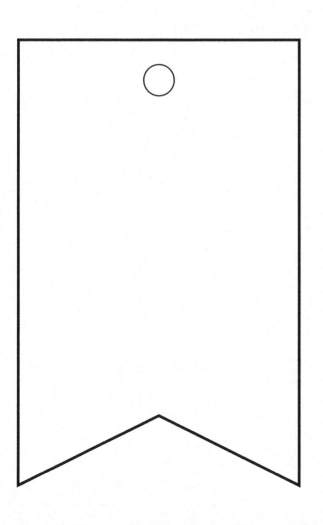

PENNANT Banner

Make a celebration banner to decorate for your party! Choose any phrase you want. Here are a few of my favorites: Celebrate, Hooray, Yay.

Practice your word with the template below, then make one on your own.

MATERIALS:
Cardstock (cut to 5.5x8.5, folded in half)
Scissors
Writing Utensil

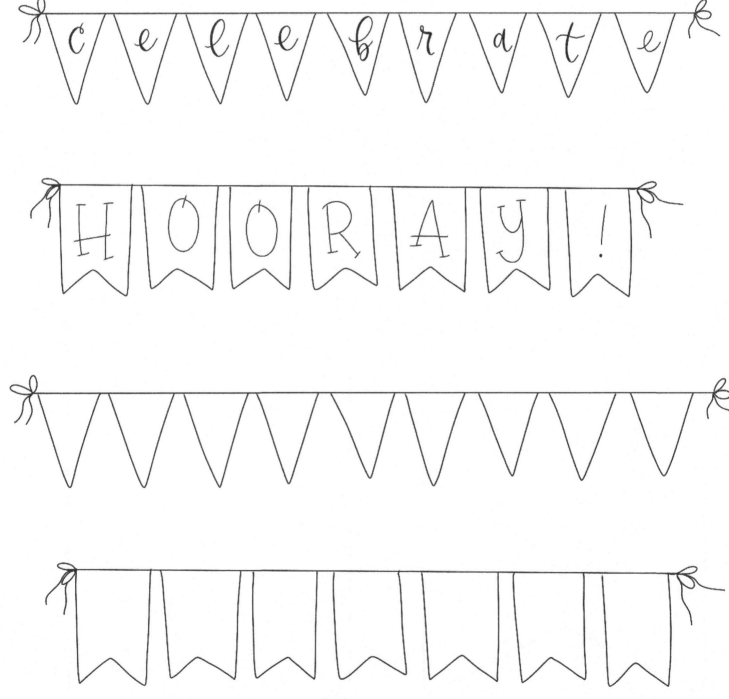

Use these templates to create your own pennant pieces out of cardstock.
Cut one for each letter of your word or phrase!

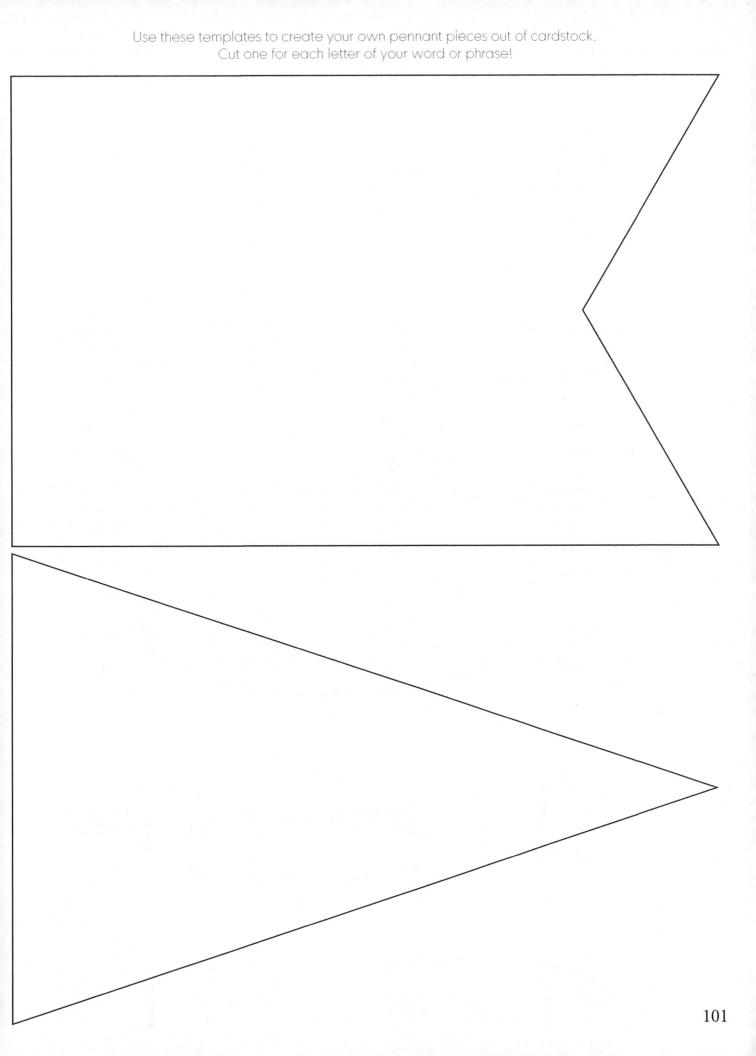

Dessert Toppers

These easy to make toppers can make a big impact on your cake, cupcakes or other dessert! Use the guidelines below to practice writing a few designs. Then create your own with the help of the templates on the next page.

MATERIALS:
Cardstock
Writing Utensil
Scissors
Toothpicks or Wooden Skewers
Tape

Pick a style below then trace onto your cardstock. Write on your word or phrase before cutting out your design. Finish it up by taping a toothpick or skewer to the back of your banner! (A single toothpick is great for small desserts like cupcakes, and a couple of longer wooden skewers are best for cakes)

PLACEMATS

Make a placemat for each guest at your party, customized with their name! Add extra doodles and patterns around their names with different colors for added fun!

MATERIALS:
Large Cardstock or Watercolor Paper
(I like to use the 11x15" paper pads that most craft stores sell)
Writing Utensil
Colored Markers

Pick a name then practice writing it on the guidelines below,
then fill the blank space with a fun pattern!

Make thank you cards to let your guests know how glad you were that they came!
Trace the design below then practice in the template at the bottom of the page.
Once you're ready, take your cardstock and get to lettering!

MATERIALS:
Cardstock (cut to 5.5x8.5, folded in half)
Scissors
Writing Utensil

Thanks so much for lettering with me! I truly hope you enjoyed the process and learned a little something along the way!

The more you practice, the more familiar your hand will get with the motions (muscle memory, right?!) and the better you will be. Remember, it's not about perfection. It's about creating something that is beautifully unique to you and you alone. Creating something out of nothing. You did that! How great are you?!

I'm really glad you picked up this book and I hope you are too! Keep on lettering and *practice practice practice!*

Made in the USA
Monee, IL
16 December 2021

85971183R00059